Your Local Area
HOMES

Ruth Thomson

Photography by Neil Thomson

WAYLAND

First published in 2010 by Wayland

Wayland
338 Euston Road
London NW1 3BH

Wayland Australia
Hachette Children's Books
Level 17/207 Kent Street
Sydney NSW 2000

Editor: Nicola Edwards
Designer: Edward Kinsey
Design Manager: Paul Cherrill

Photographic credits
All photographs in this book, except those listed below, were taken by Neil Thomson. p14 (top left): Bobby Humphey/Discovery/ Franklin Watts; page 15 (top centre): Andy Crawford.

British Library Cataloguing in Publication Data

Thomson, Ruth, 1949-
  Your local area.
  Homes.
  1. Dwellings--Juvenile literature. 2. Housing--Juvenile literature.
  I. Title
  307.3'36-dc22

ISBN 978 0 7502 6083 1

Printed in China

Wayland is a division of Hachette Children's Books, a Hachette UK Company.
www. hachette.co.uk

Free downloadable material is available to complement the activities in the Your Local Area series, including worksheets, templates for charts and photographic identification charts. For more information go to:
www.waylandbooks.co.uk/yourlocalarea
<http://www.waylandbooks.co.uk/yourlocalarea>

Contents

What is a home?

Homes are places where people can live, sheltered from the sun, wind and rain. Most homes have separate rooms for sleeping, washing, cooking and relaxing. They have places where people can store their belongings.

All homes have some common features, whatever their size, shape or style.

A roof protects a home from all weathers.

Walls enclose the space and hold up the roof.

A front door is the way in and out.

Windows let in light and air.

A local look

★ What is the same about these homes and what differences can you spot?

A bungalow is one storey high. It has no staircase. All the rooms are on the ground floor.

Semi-detached houses are two houses joined as a pair.

Flats are homes stacked one on top of the other in the same building. The rooms in a flat are all on one floor.

Terraced houses are joined together in a row.

A detached house stands all by itself. It is not joined to any other house.

★ **Take a walk around your area and see which type of home is the most common.**
★ **Draw or photograph the different types of house you see.**

Where are homes?

People live in cities, towns, villages, in the country or by the sea. Towns and cities are built-up with streets of houses, shops and offices. Suburbs on the edge of cities are mainly housing. Most suburban homes have gardens.

? **What differences do you notice between the suburban street (above) and the city view (below)?**

Villages are small settlements that have grown up over hundreds of years. The houses often cluster around a green, a church or a square.

Farmhouses usually stand on their own. They are surrounded by fields where farmers grow crops or graze cattle or sheep.

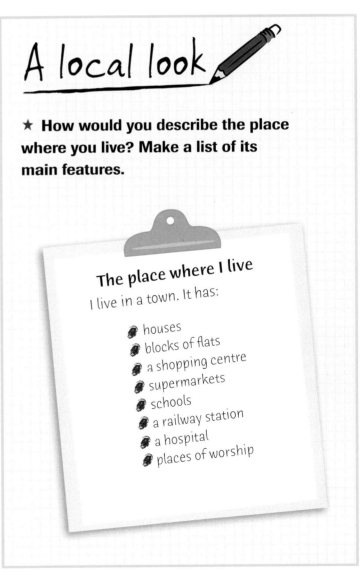

A local look

★ **How would you describe the place where you live? Make a list of its main features.**

The place where I live

I live in a town. It has:

- houses
- blocks of flats
- a shopping centre
- supermarkets
- schools
- a railway station
- a hospital
- places of worship

Around your home

Most homes are not far from a local shop and café. Some have nearby bus or train services. Local public places, such as parks, swimming pools, playgrounds and libraries, can all help make an area a pleasant place to live.

park

bus service

What do you have near where you live?

café

food shop

SIGN OF THE PAST

Old statues, drinking fountains, clocks, war memorials and water pumps are often local landmarks.

★ **What landmarks are there in your area?**

drinking fountain

statue

clock

A local look

★ **Which of these things do you think might be nice or nasty in an area?**

★ **Photograph things that you think are nice or nasty around your home.**

allotments

street art

tree-lined street

playground

graffiti

vandalism

dog mess

bench

underpass

Up your street

Most houses are built along a street. Depending upon where you live, the streets may be narrow or wide, long or short. Some lead to other streets, while others have a dead end, called a cul de sac. Blocks of flats are usually surrounded by a patch of green space.

A local look

Think of ways you could improve the way a local street looks and feels.

★ Is there much litter? Where is it mostly found?
★ Are there any litter or recycling bins? Is there a space to put some?

★ Is there anywhere to sit? Where would you put a bench if you had the chance?

★ **Design a mural or a sculpture to brighten up your street.**

Streetlights on the pavements light up streets at night. They come on at dusk and go off at dawn.

★ **Are there trees, plants, grass verges or flowerbeds in the street? Where could you put or hang some plants?**

SIGN OF THE PAST

Post boxes first appeared on streets in Victorian times after the invention of postage stamps. This post box has the intials VR, short for Victoria Regina (regina is the Latin word for queen).

Traffic near homes

The noise, pollution and danger of busy traffic can spoil areas where people live. Local councils have found ways to make sure that residential streets are as quiet and safe as possible.

 Why is a zebra crossing a safe place to cross the road?

A local look

Notice how traffic is controlled in the streets around your home.

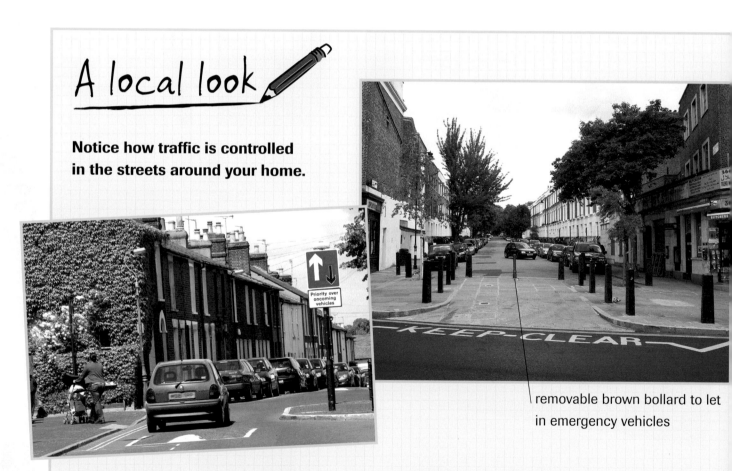

Priority over oncoming vehicles

KEEP CLEAR

removable brown bollard to let in emergency vehicles

★ **Have any roads been narrowed to stop big trucks from coming in?**
★ **Do any have speed humps to slow down traffic?**

★ **Have any residential streets been blocked off from a main road?**
★ **What instructions or orders do the road markings give?**

Parking is controlled in residential areas in towns and cities. This helps make the roads quieter and residents can park near their homes. Speed signs remind drivers to slow down.

★ **Look for signs, markings and other features like these, that help control the speed of cars on residential streets.**

20 miles an hour road marking

white arrows to show where a speed hump is

speed hump

20 miles an hour zone road sign

barrier to protect pedestrians

road narrowing

a change in the colour and texture of the road to remind drivers to slow down

Your address

Every home has a name or a number so that the postman, visitors and deliveries can find the right address.

A local look

★ Record how people number or name their homes.
★ Design a name plaque for your own home.

12A
12B
12C

THE LITTLE HOUSE

SIXTY FOUR

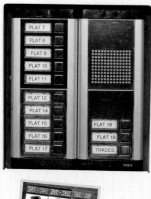

FLAT 7
FLAT 8
FLAT 9
FLAT 10
FLAT 11
FLAT 12
FLAT 14
FLAT 15   FLAT 18
FLAT 16   FLAT 19
FLAT 17   TRADES

105

SIGN OF THE PAST

The Hayloft

The name of a home can give a clue about who once lived there or what the building was used for in the past.

★ Visit your local studies library or museum to find out about the history of the buildings.

School Cottage

WEAVER'S COTTAGE

When people send you a letter, they write your name and address on it, so the post office knows where to deliver it.

 Can you write out your own address? Put your name, your street, your town or village and your country each on a different line.

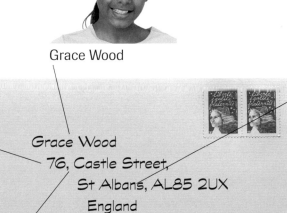

Grace Wood

town, city or village

house number

Grace Wood
76, Castle Street,
St Albans, AL85 2UX
England

ENGLAND

CASTLE STREET

street

country

Can you find any old door knockers? Why did people use knockers in the past instead of doorbells?

Before postage stamps were invented in 1840, the person who received a letter paid for it. Once postmen started delivering letters, people fitted letter boxes in their front doors, so postmen did not have to knock. You can still find Victorian letter boxes.

Marking your space

There is always a clear boundary dividing the private spaces of homes from the public pavement or road. This is often marked by a wall, a hedge or a fence.

 How are the boundaries between these houses and the pavement marked?

Some houses open straight on to the street. Their boundary is the front door.

Some people extend their boundary by putting flower pots on the pavement outside their house or by planting their own flowers around trees on the roadside.

A local look

gates

★ Carry out a survey in a nearby street to see how many different ways people have marked the boundaries of their space.

★ What is the most common boundary?

Boundary markers

gates	⦀⦀⦀ |||
walls	⦀⦀⦀ ||
fences	⦀⦀⦀	
hedges	||||
plants	||

low wall   fences

hedges

plants

Home sweet home

Look around to see how people make their homes different from one another. Notice whether they have changed a feature of the building or made a show of plants or ornaments in their front gardens.

People who live in flats sometimes turn their balconies into a garden.

? How have people made these houses different?

 These two semi-detached houses were originally built looking exactly the same. What differences can you spot between them?

A local look

★ Take photographs of houses that stand out. What makes them different from their neighbours?

★ Look at a street where the houses have front gardens. Which one do you think most deserves a garden prize?

★ People often change their front doors. Look at doors in a street with the same sort of houses. How do the front doors differ? Draw the one you like best.

Building materials

Homes are made of hard, waterproof materials. In Britain, most homes are built of brick. Some are made with natural materials, such as stone and slate. Other materials, such as glass, wood, metal and plastic are used for different parts of a house.

? How do the stone walls of this house differ from brick walls?

baked clay roof tiles

baked clay brick walls

plastic window frames with glass panes

a wooden door with glass panels and a metal letterbox

? What materials is your home made of?

A local look

Brickwork patterns are called bonds.
★ **Record different bonds in your area.**

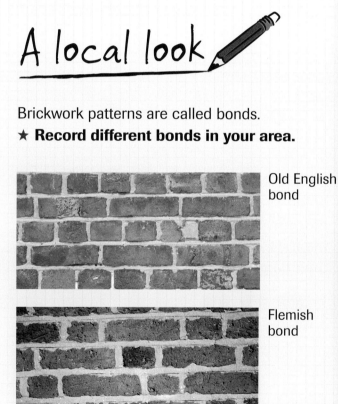

Old English bond

Flemish bond

Stretcher bond

★ **How do these bonds differ?**

Hundreds of years ago, people built with the closest local stone, such as limestone, sandstone, flint or granite.

flint house

limestone cottage

In some places there was plenty of wood. Builders made a timber frame with walls of plaited sticks, clay and dung, known as wattle and daub.

In other places, people built houses of cob. This is a mixture of mud, dung and straw. The roof is made of straw thatch.

Old and new houses

Victorian houses are the old homes you will see most often. You can still find rows of terraced houses near town centres and large, detached houses, called villas, in the suburbs or at the seaside. New blocks of flats have been built in many city centres, but modern houses are more often built in their suburbs.

Victorian terrace

A local look

★ **Find a Victorian house to draw. Label its main features.**

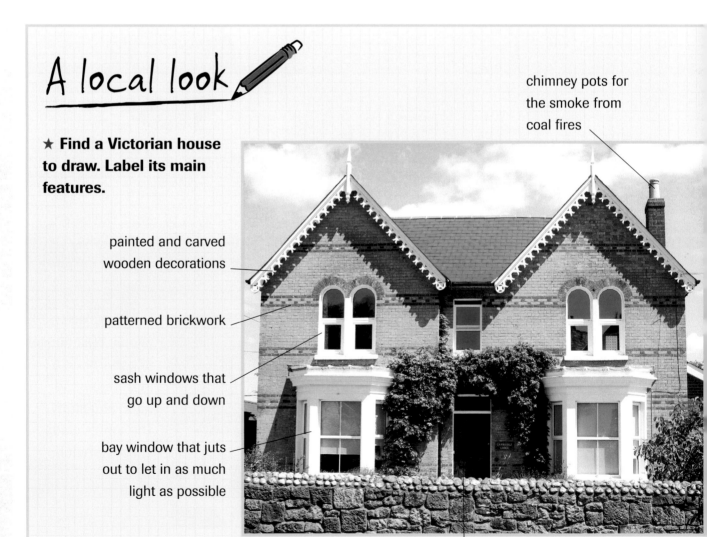

chimney pots for the smoke from coal fires

painted and carved wooden decorations

patterned brickwork

sash windows that go up and down

bay window that juts out to let in as much light as possible

door with glass panels

Very modern houses sometimes have windows with huge panes of glass.

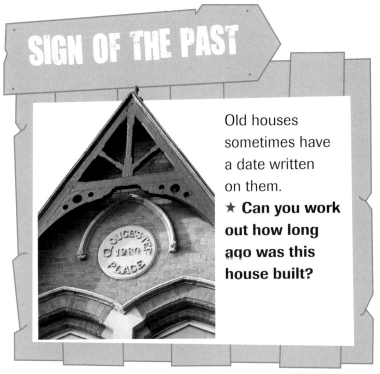

Old houses sometimes have a date written on them.
★ **Can you work out how long ago was this house built?**

★ **List the similarities and differences you notice between the Victorian house and this modern one.**

no chimneys on the roof

windows usually double-glazed to keep house warmer and quieter

built-in garage for a car

Services

Homes are connected to a network of services. They have electricity for lighting, water for baths, loos and kitchens, and gas or electricity for cooking and heating. Most homes also have a TV and a telephone.

 Why can't you usually see water pipes like these ?

Refuse collectors take away waste. They often collect glass, paper, metal, food and garden waste separately for recycling.

 What things are collected for recycling in your area?

SIGN OF THE PAST

Victorians used coal as fuel for cooking, as well as for heating rooms and water. Coal was tipped into cellars through holes in the pavement.

★ **Look for coal hole covers on the pavement outside Victorian houses. Take a rubbing of one.**

A local look

Gas and water pipes and electricity cables run under the street. Metal covers in the pavement show where these are.

You can often see telephone wires and TV aerials fixed to walls or roofs.

★ **Take a walk along your street and take photographs of the services you can spot.**

The services in my home

my bedroom
- light
- lamp

bathroom
- lights
- basin bath or shower

living room
- lights
- computer

kitchen
- lights
- toaster
- sink
- cooker

colour key to services
- electricity
- water
- gas

★ **Draw a plan of some rooms in your home. Write or draw the services you can find in each room. Include a colour key.**

Unusual homes

Over time, people change the way they use buildings. All over the country, builders have turned old farm buildings, factories, warehouses, chapels, mills, schools and railways stations into houses or flats.

SIGN OF THE PAST

When builders convert old buildings into houses, they often leave features, such as doors, windows, pulleys and chimneys. These give clues to the original use of the building.

pulley used for lifting and lowering sacks

? What clues tell you that this house was once a barn? What clues show that this is now a house?

These buildings were once part of a maltings. This is where workers turned barley into malt for brewing beer.

 What clues tell you that these buildings are now homes?

A local look

★ **Find an old building in your area that has been changed into a home. Sketch or take photographs of interesting features.**

★ **Decide which features are original and which are new. Make a chart like this to record your findings.**

birdfeeder

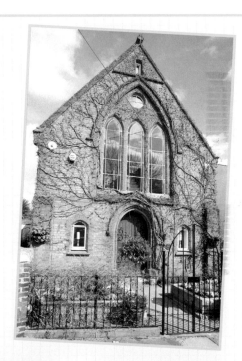
chapel

A chapel turned into a house

Original features
- large upstairs windows
- arched wooden door with metal hinges
- two colour brickwork

New features
- metal railings
- metal gate
- burglar alarm
- raised flowerbeds
- hanging baskets
- bird feeder
- house nameplate
- flower pots

house nameplate

door and flower pots

More things to do

Get to know the homes in your area better by taking a close look at their details. Record these in drawings and photographs.

★ Does every house have chimneys – one, two, lots or none?

★ Notice changes that people have made to houses. Look for new rooms, such as a loft or conservatory, porches or windows different from houses nearby.

★ Draw or photograph different windows. Work out how they open and close. Count their panes.

Window shapes

conservatory

enclosed porch

★ **Make a map of your area.**
★ **Shade housing in one colour, shops n another and open spaces in green.**
★ **Mark bus stops, railway lines and bridges.**
★ **Mark any places to eat and drink.**

★ **Mark buildings, such as a library or village hall with symbols. Invent your own symbols and include a key to show what they mean.**
★ **Mark where your home is.**

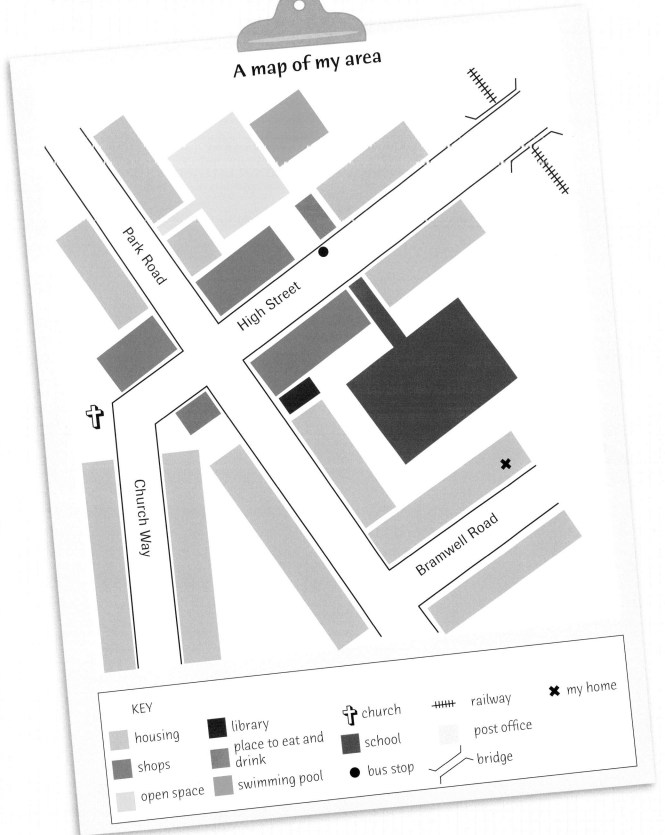

A map of my area

Park Road

High Street

Church Way

Bramwell Road

KEY

housing
shops
open space

library
place to eat and drink
swimming pool

✝ church
school
● bus stop

┼┼┼┼ railway
post office
bridge

✖ my home

Glossary

balcony a platform on the outer wall of a building, with a wall or railings around it

boundary a line dividing a place from the place next to it

bungalow a house with only one floor

cables wires that electricity and telephone messages are carried through

chapel a small church

detached house a house that stands all by itself

double glazing windows with two layers of glass with air in-between, that keep homes warmer and quieter

mural a picture painted directly on to a wall

ornament an object used to decorate something

private belonging to only one person or small group

public for all the people of a place

pulley a device with a wheel and a rope used for lifting and lowering loads

resident someone who lives in a place

residential area an area made up of housing rather then shops, offices or factories

semi-detached joined to another house on one side

settlement a place where people arrived and set up their homes

suburb an area of houses on the outer edges of towns and cities

symbol a sign used to mean something, for example the symbol = means equals

terrace a row of houses joined to one another

verge a grassy area by the side of a road

Victorian the time when Queen Victoria ruled Britain – from 1837 to 1901

villa a large house

warehouse a large building where businesses store their goods

war memorial something put up to remember people who died in a war

Talking points

The questions in the book encourage close observation of the pictures and provide talking points for discussion.

Pages 4-5
The main differences between the types of homes are:
the position and decoration of the front door
the number, shape and size of the windows
the existence (or not) and number of chimneys
the existence of porches
the roofline
the number of storeys (floors)
the building materials and colour.

Page 6
The main differences between the suburban road and the city view are:
the suburban houses are detached and more widely spaced apart, whereas the terraced city houses are packed closely together
the suburban road is wide and curved, whereas the city street is narrow and straight
the suburban road is greener with tall trees and shrubs, whereas the city street has very little greenery
the suburban houses are more modern than the city houses and set further back from the pavement
the suburban houses have driveways for cars; the cars in the city are parked on both sides of the street
the city view shows shops, a church and a park at the bottom of the hill.

Page 8
Nice things are the allotments, the tree-lined street, the bench and the playground. Nasty things are the possibility of dog mess, vandalism, graffiti, the rows of cars parked along the sides of the street and the underpass. Whether street art is nice or nasty is a discussion point!

Pages 10-11
Compare the arrangement of houses and blocks of flats. Houses are arranged in a line along a street. The blocks of flats are spaced widely apart with a large area of green around them.

Page 12
Drivers must stop for pedestrians on a zebra crossing. The black and white lines on the road and the flashing orange Belisha beacons remind drivers to slow down.

Page 15
Victorian used knockers instead of doorbells because electricity had not yet been discovered.

Pages 16-17
People have marked their boundaries with:
• a huge arched hedge and a low wall
• a low wall and a crazy-paved driveway
• iron railings and a gate.

Page 19
People made their homes different by painting the outside walls and front doors in a variety of colours.

The differences between the semi-detached houses are:
• the colour of the outside walls
• the number of panes of glass on the windows
• the windows of the left-hand house have shutters
• one has a glass front door, the other door is wooden
• the left-hand house has a garage and balcony
• the left-hand house has pillars, railings and gates on the boundary wall, whereas the other has only a low wall
• plants grow outside the door of the left-hand house.

Pages 20-21
Stone walls include stones of different sizes and shapes, whereas bricks are all the same size and shape.

Pages 22-23
• Both the Victorian and modern house are built of brick in two contrasting colours; have sloping roofs, front walls that meet at a point and front doors with two glass panels
• The Victorian house has chimneys, bay and arched windows, and carved decorations. The modern house has a garage and driveway, a porch, a window in the roof and no chimneys.

Page 24
You cannot usually see water pipes (or gas pipes and electricity cables), because they are hidden under the street.

Pages 26-27
• The house still has the original barn door opening and shutters and slit windows along the side that show it was once a barn. It has a new windows and a front door with a hanging lantern at the front, and a letterbox outside to show it is now a house.
• The curtains at the windows, the shrubs that separate the entrance to different houses and the balconies all show that the maltings are now homes.

Index